T0015966

# POCKET HOTTIES

# PEDRO PASCAL

## INSPIRATIONAL QUOTES AND OBSERVATIONS ON LIFE

Independently authored and published. This work is not associated with or authorized by Pedro Pascal.

Copyright © 2023 Ulysses Press and its licensors. All rights reserved. Any unauthorized duplication in whole or in part or dissemination of this edition by any means (including but not limited to photocopying, electronic devices, digital versions, and the internet) will be prosecuted to the fullest extent of the law.

Published by:
Uysses Press
PO Box 3440
Berkeley, CA 94703
www.ulyssespress.com

ISBN: 978-1-64604-646-1

Printed in India
10 9 8 7 6 5 4 3 2 1

Acquisitions editor: Claire Sielaff
Managing editor: Claire Chun
Editors: Barbara Schultz, Renee Rutledge
Design and layout: Winnie Liu

NOTE TO READERS: This book is independently authored and published and no sponsorship or endorsement of this book by, and no affiliation with, Pedro Pascal or any other celebrities, shows, movies, characters, or trademarked products mentioned within is claimed or suggested. All celebrities, shows, movies, characters, or trademarked products that appear in this book belong to their respective owners and are used here for informational purposes only. The author and publisher encourage readers to patronize the shows, movies, and other products mentioned in this book.

RELATIONSHIPS

# RELATIONSHIPS

"

My protective side is lethal.

"

# RELATIONSHIPS

"

I got an entire New York family
through them [LaGuardia High
alums], to the point where they
still forget I didn't actually go
to high school with them.

"

---

*Esquire*, April 11, 2023

# RELATIONSHIPS

"

I just always wanted to
be like, *I'm here.*

"

---

In regard to feeling parental
toward his younger siblings,
*Esquire*, April 11, 2023

# RELATIONSHIPS

"

I love you. I miss you. Thank
you. I'm scared. I would love it
if you would help me believe in
myself, because I know you do.

"

----------------------------------------

In regard to his late mother,
*Esquire*, April 11, 2023

# RELATIONSHIPS

"

My siblings and my chosen family
are where I invest all of my emotional
energy. But I'm also a little protective
of people's experience in general.

"

*Esquire*, April 11, 2023

# RELATIONSHIPS

"

His head got bigger than his ears!

"

Joking about Grogu,
*The Tonight Show Starring Jimmy
Fallon*, YouTube, February 3, 2023

# RELATIONSHIPS

"

There's thirty-four first cousins.

"

# RELATIONSHIPS

"

I tell my family everything.

"

Variety, YouTube, June 9, 2021

# HIMSELF

# HIMSELF

**"**

Invite me over [...] we'll
have a good time.

**"**

# HIMSELF

"

A lot of people have my phone number. I definitely gave it out way too much over the years.

"

# HIMSELF

"

Daddy is a state of mind, you know
what I'm saying? I'm your daddy.

"

# HIMSELF

"

I am your cool, slutty daddy.

"

-------------------------------------------------

*Entertainment Tonight*, YouTube, January 17, 2023

**14**

# HIMSELF

"

I tried to play the game, and
I was very, very bad at it.

"

---

On *The Last of Us*,
*Wired*, January 9, 2023

# HIMSELF

"

Why am I trying to force a
square shape into a triangle?

"

*Esquire*, April 11, 2023

# HIMSELF

"

I didn't get into any physical
fights growing up, and definitely
not as an adult. Violence
scares me tremendously.

"

# HIMSELF

"

I just don't want to make
any decisions.

"

# HIMSELF

"

I love thrill-seeking stuff. But I
don't make a practice of testing
my limits. I'm actually a little bit
opposed to it. I don't like pain.

"

# HIMSELF

"

Come see about me, leave me
alone, come see about me, leave me
alone. That's my catchphrase.

"

*Esquire*, April 11, 2023

# HIMSELF

"

I need a new mattress before
I can buy a football team.

"

# HIMSELF

"

I want people to feel comfortable.
I don't know how to function at
the expense of anyone's comfort
level. I'm a people pleaser.

"

# HIMSELF

"
Daddy Pascal ... Papi Pascal.
"

# HIMSELF

"

The reason my older sister and I grew up in the States is because my parents fled a military dictatorship.

"

# HIMSELF

"

I would say that I am a Chilean,
Texan, Californian, New Yorker.

"

# HIMSELF

"

My ... astonishing mustache.

"

# HIMSELF

"
I'm not a very good sleeper.
"

*First We Feast*, YouTube, March 9, 2023

# HIMSELF

"

I need people to like me, you
know what I mean?

"

# HIMSELF

"

I'm 5'11".

"

# HIMSELF

"

Now people are like ... don't ever
get rid of your mustache. You look
like my grandmother without it.

"

# HIMSELF

"

I wanna go from Daddy back to Baby.

"

# HIMSELF

"

I tried to change my name so that I
could get more work […] I changed
my name to Alexander Pascal […]
There was like a kind of shadow of
discomfort to that entire year until
I just changed it back to Pedro.

"

Google Play, YouTube, September 29, 2017

# LIFE

"

If my parents liked what they were watching, they rarely sent me out of the room. But I had to get good grades or I wasn't allowed to watch shit.

"

# LIFE

"

I want to take care of people as
much as they took care of me.

"

# LIFE

"

Everywhere is home and nowhere
is home. But that also still feels
like a good thing to me.

"

*Wired*, January 9, 2023

# LIFE

"

I'm relinquishing expectations
around what it is to be middle-
aged and what it means
to be fully grown up.

"

---

*Esquire*, April 11, 2023

"

I'm a Chileno, gringo, according
to my enormous family.

"

-------------------------------------------------

# LIFE

"

I fucking hate milk.

"

*First We Feast*, YouTube, March 9, 2023

# LIFE

"

I didn't go to church. I was raised
by HBO, Spielberg, and Prince.

"

*First We Feast*, YouTube, March 9, 2023

# LIFE

"

What does it all mean? I'll tell
you. I don't know. And I don't
think we're supposed to. And
that's the meaning of life.

"

*Entertainment Tonight*, YouTube, March 1, 2023

# LIFE

"

I am a child of socialist political
refugees. We are very, very liberal.

"

*The Late Show with Stephen Colbert*,
YouTube, August 30, 2016

# LIFE

"

I am an Aries sun. […] And then there's
a debate because I can't seem to track
down my birth certificate. […] So I'm
either Gemini rising or Cancer rising,
but I know I have Capricorn moon.

"

# LIFE

"

I was a waiter for about seven
years and it started early and
I got fired from, I don't know,
maybe upwards of like twenty to
thirty restaurants in New York
City within those seven years.

"

Facebook Live, uploaded by BigFatSexyCat@
YouTube, April 26, 2018

# LIFE

"

I'm sort of set in my ways. I've lived
in New York for a really long time.

"

Google Play, YouTube, September 29, 2017

# LIFE

"

I'm usually not all that interested
in challenging myself.

"

---

*Esquire*, April 11, 2023

**46**

# LIFE

"

My vision of it was that if I didn't
have some major exposure by the
time I was twenty-nine years old,
it was over, so I was constantly
readjusting what it meant to
commit my life to this profession.

"

# SUCCESS

# SUCCESS

"

I feel good when people recognize
me. Sometimes I feel surprised.

"

Google Play, YouTube, September 29, 2017

# SUCCESS

"

What's next? I have no fucking idea.

"

# SUCCESS

"

I just hope that I have the maturity
to not chase something that would
mean more from the outside.

"

*Esquire*, April 11, 2023

# SUCCESS

"

You forgot *Law and Order: SVU.*

"

In regard to his list of acting credits,
*The Tonight Show Starring Jimmy
Fallon,* YouTube, February 3, 2023

# SUCCESS

"

I got my head crushed in. It
was the best part of the day.

"

In regard to filming *Game of Thrones* (GOT),
*First We Feast*, YouTube, March 9, 2023

# SUCCESS

"

Oberyn mother-fucking Martell,
man! [...] Changed my life!

"

# SUCCESS

"

It was amazing. Just very surreal,
cuz I was also stepping onto the set
of a show that I was obsessed with.

"

---

In regard to filming *GOT*,
*GQ*, YouTube, March 14, 2019

# SUCCESS

"

I had to stop myself from
asking for autographs.

"

---------------------------------------------------

On filming *Kingsman: The Golden Circle*,
*GQ*, YouTube, March 14, 2019

# SUCCESS

"

I hadn't been so afraid of not getting
a job as this one in so many years
because I've been hustling for so long.

"

On getting cast in *Kingsman:
The Golden Circle*,
Google Play, YouTube, September 22, 2017

# SOCIETY AND CULTURE

# SOCIETY AND CULTURE

"

My entire heart is set on, you
know, the marginalized underdog.
It's not a choice. Like, how dare
anyone not support the people
that are deserving of support,
and are deserving of protection
and need more of it than you do.

"

*Wired*, January 9, 2023

"

There's a lot of content.
It's easy to avoid me.

"

--------------------------------------------------

Joking about appearing in
many famous shows,
Capital FM, YouTube, March 2, 2023

# SOCIETY AND CULTURE

"

To comfort myself, I just
remember that everybody I come
in contact with is sort of, in their
own way, heroically kind.

"

"

I feel somewhat at home no matter where I go in Latin America. Even if they think I'm an uptight Chileno!

"

-----

Google Play, YouTube, September 29, 2017

# SOCIETY AND CULTURE

"

There's so many ways to
misunderstand people and to
forget that, at the end of the day,
your neighbor is very likely to give
you the shirt off their own back.

"

---------------------------------------------

*Wired*, January 9, 2023

"

Cap'n Crunch is just so tasty.

"

"

For me, 'Purple Rain' is like the most emotionally cathartic, the most musically sophisticated song.

"

"

I think I'm gonna go to the
Whitney museum this afternoon,
unless I, uh, shit myself.

"

---

In regard to post-*Hot Ones* plans,
*First We Feast*, YouTube, March 9, 2023

# SOCIETY AND CULTURE

"

I love TikTok.

"

Capital FM, YouTube, March 2, 2023

# SOCIETY AND CULTURE

"

My FYP continues to be cooking
and hilarious, dark-humor
fails, and all kinds of comedy.

"

Capital FM, YouTube, March 2, 2023

# SOCIETY AND CULTURE

"

I can connect myself to what is
a Latin American immigrant
experience or first-generation
American experience
from Latin America.

"

Google Play, YouTube, September 22, 2017

# SOCIETY AND CULTURE

"

This [Reese's Peanut Butter Cup]
is my favorite chocolate bar.
[...] Reese's beats all for me.

"

---

*LADbible TV*, YouTube, March 1, 2023

# SOCIETY AND CULTURE

"

Peanut butter is really good.

"

# SOCIETY AND CULTURE

"

This is not the way. Apologies to
whoever eats pineapple on pizza.

"

# SOCIETY AND CULTURE

"

Our experience as immigrants
in the U.S. meant really
diving into pop culture.

"

Google Play, YouTube, September 29, 2017

# SOCIETY AND CULTURE

"

Gosh ... there are so many daddies.
Let's give it to Oscar Isaac.

"

In regard to what other actor
should be called "Daddy,"
MTV UK, YouTube, February 24, 2023

# SOCIETY AND CULTURE

"

When I really really love something,
even if the entire thing is available
to me, I sparse it out. I'll do no
more than two episodes at a time
[...] because I like to savor things.

"

# SOCIETY AND CULTURE

"

I would say my cultural
identity is a very interesting
question to try to answer.

"

Google Play, YouTube, September 29, 2017

# SOCIETY AND CULTURE

"

My advice to young Hispanic
artists would be […] be yourself.
And make that your complete
priority. Do not compromise
anything that is true to yourself
to meet some exterior standard.

"

Google Play, YouTube, September 29, 2017

# ACTING

# ACTING

"

That's the fun part   how much you
get to externalize internal darkness
in a safe way and bring in things
that are from your nightmares.

"

# ACTING

"

I realize that I'm doing something
and I'm saying something in a way
that I have to stop and take a second
and realize, 'Oh I got that from
*Vampire's Kiss*,' or something.

"

---

In regard to taking inspiration
from Nicolas Cage,
*First We Feast*, YouTube, March 9, 2023

# ACTING

"

There was a really, really unusually fun character that I played on *NYPD Blue*, this goth guy named Dio.

"

# ACTING

"

If you watch *Law and Order*,
all three of them, I always
die on *Law and Order*.

"

---

*Wired*, YouTube, March 12, 2019

# ACTING

"

[*The Good Wife*] was maybe one
of my first recurring roles.

"

*GQ*, YouTube, March 14, 2019

# ACTING

"

That show is amazing, it's one of my favorite shows. I continued watching it long after I was an afterthought.

"

---

In regard to *The Good Wife*,
*GQ*, YouTube, March 14, 2019

# ACTING

"

That may literally be the very
first secret that I've ever kept.

"

---

In regard to Grogu,
*Variety*, YouTube, June 9, 2021

# ACTING

"

I started my career off in New
York, and theater is my home.

"

# ACTING

**"**

Ironically [...] there's a chance
that [...] the superfan that Javi is
a lot closer to me than maybe the
Nic Cage in this movie is to the
Nicolas Cage that played him.

**"**

---

In regard to *The Unbearable
Weight of Massive Talent*,
*Digital Spy*, YouTube, April 17 2022

# ACTING

"

Weirdly this is more myself
than so many other things
that I may be known for.

"

---------------------------------------------------

In regard to *The Unbearable
Weight of Massive Talent,*
*Digital Spy,* YouTube, April 17 2022

# ACTING

"

My agent told me that, 'The director,
Matthew Vaughn, has you in mind
for a role in the second *Kingsman*.'
And I didn't believe him because
I was actually kind of depressed
that day and I thought he was
just trying to [...] cheer me up.

"

Google Play, YouTube, September 22, 2017

# ACTING

"

I did a little bit more training with
the whip because I enjoyed the
whip more than I did the other
things—or I was better at it.

"

In regard to training for
*Kingsman: The Golden Circle,*
Google Play, YouTube, September 22, 2017

# ACTING

"

[Typecasting] is an interesting
symptom of an industry.

"

Google Play, YouTube, September 29, 2017

# ACTING

"
I think that today's greatest living
director is Alfonso Cuarón.
"

Google Play, YouTube, September 29, 2017

# ACTING

"

Turns out, I became an actor
and I would say seeing a lot
of Nicolas Cage's movies
had a lot to do with why.

"

*ScreenSlam*, YouTube, April 9, 2022

# ACTING

"

I guess on [*Game of Thrones*] I was learning what makes me nervous and what doesn't. The dirty stuff didn't make me that nervous.

"

*Opie & Anthony Show* interview from February 17, 2014, posted by foundry archives @ YouTube, March 26, 2020